MOVING TO THE UAE:
A COMPLETE GUIDE

Emma Coffey

Copyright © 2023 Moving to the UAE: A Complete Guide

All rights reserved. No part of this publication may be reproduced, distributed, or transmitted in any form or by any means, including photocopying, recording, or other electronic or mechanical methods, without the prior written permission of the publisher, except in the case of brief quotations embodied in critical reviews and certain other noncommercial uses permitted by copyright law.

Printed by Amazon, Inc., in the United States of America.

First printing edition 2023.

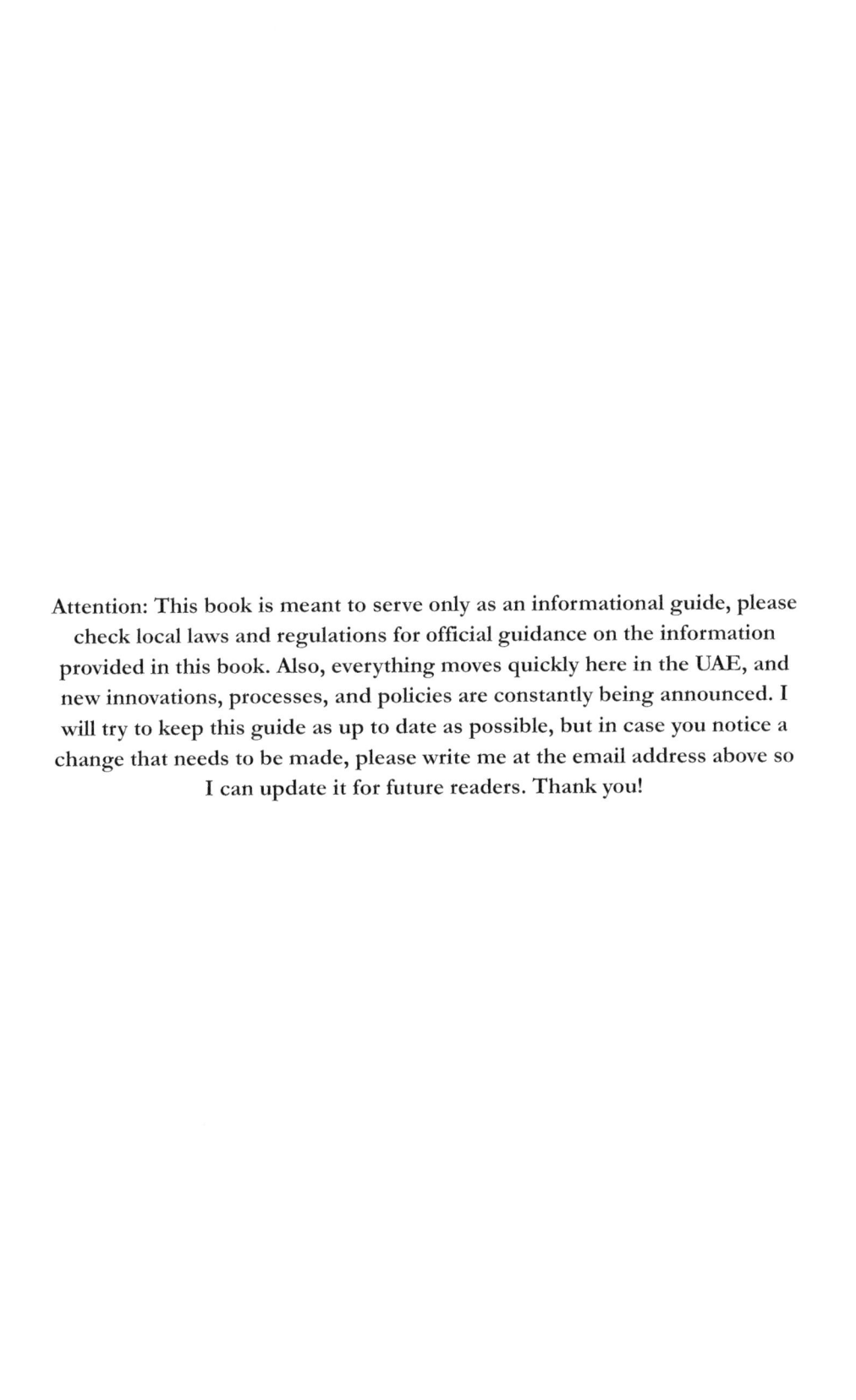

Attention: This book is meant to serve only as an informational guide, please check local laws and regulations for official guidance on the information provided in this book. Also, everything moves quickly here in the UAE, and new innovations, processes, and policies are constantly being announced. I will try to keep this guide as up to date as possible, but in case you notice a change that needs to be made, please write me at the email address above so I can update it for future readers. Thank you!

TABLE OF CONTENTS

Introduction 7
Chapter 1: Before You Leave..9
Chapter 2: Your First Days..18
Chapter 3: Choosing Where To Live..21
Chapter 4: Government Documents 28
Chapter 5: Banking 35
Chapter 6: Phone Plans 39
Chapter 7: Searching For a Place To Live 41
Chapter 8: Utilities and Bills 48
Chapter 9: Getting Around..52
Chapter 10: Local Customs and Culture 60
Chapter 11: Moving With Your Family 65
Chapter 12: Health 71
Chapter 13: Tips and Tricks 74
Index 82
Emergency Numbers in the UAE...85

INTRODUCTION

Ahlan wa sahlan! Welcome! As an expat who moved to the United Arab Emirates a number of years ago, it was quite a long journey getting my feet on the ground and trying to learn everything there was to learn about my new home.

I have been informally compiling list after list to help friends and acquaintances who move here, and wanted to share my learnings with others, in the hopes that it might help someone else that is considering (or already planning) a move to the country.

The United Arab Emirates is a wonderful place to live, with kind people and a fascinating cultural tapestry to explore. And with over 90% of the country made up of expats from around the world, you should have no trouble finding a community for yourself.

So good luck, and I hope that you will find this information useful as you settle into your new home. If you have any feedback or other information to share with new people moving to the area, please do not hesitate to contact me by email at movingtotheuae@gmail.com.

Wishing you the best of luck on this new adventure!

CHAPTER 1

BEFORE YOU LEAVE

Whether you already have a job lined up, or you have decided to take the plunge and figure things out when you get there, there are a number of considerations you will need to think about before you set off.

Initial checklist

Before you leave, there are a number of steps you should take in order to make your transition as smooth as possible. A few of these considerations include:

☐ Check your passport validity to ensure that it will not expire in the next six months

- ☐ Inform your bank you are moving to the UAE and ensure that you can access your accounts from abroad

- ☐ Prepare key documentation such as your home driver's license, rental references, school documents for children, and pet health records

- ☐ Consider moving insurance to protect your household goods (this is not an absolute necessity but it is always better to be safe than sorry)

- ☐ Pay your final bills from your home country

- ☐ Find a shipping company you trust and inform yourself about what you can and cannot bring into the country

- ☐ Make a plan for your taxes, depending on how it works in your home country

- ☐ Understand if you need to submit vaccinations or a health check before you arrive

- ☐ Make a plan to have health insurance if it is not going to be provided by your employer or sponsor

- ☐ Redirect your mail to someone you trust

Visas

Before arriving in the UAE, you will need a plan for how to stay there (beyond a tourist visa of course). There are many options, but I will cover the most common routes that people take.

1. Company-sponsored visa: This is the most common type of visa, and to get it you will need to make sure that you have a company who has agreed to sponsor you *before* you arrive, that you have signed an offer letter from the company, and that they have issued you an entry permit to travel to the UAE.

2. Job-seeker visa: This is a brand-new type of visa that was announced in 2022, it allows people without sponsorship to come into the UAE to search for work, investment or business opportunities, for a limited time.

3. Family-sponsored visa: Spouses and children are allowed to be sponsored by someone that has a company-sponsored visa (with certain restrictions), or if they are an investor, business owner, or property owner in the UAE.

4. Golden visa: This is a rather new offering from the UAE Government that allows eligible visa holders to maintain residency in the UAE for up to ten years, and to sponsor their family members, spouse, children, and support staff. Only some professions

are eligible for the visa, which includes people that have made contributions in the fields of: cultures and art, investors and innovators, sports, digital technology, humanitarianism, and other fields (new fields are added frequently and the rules are also updated often).

5. Green visa: This is another new offering from the UAE Government which provides visa holders and their first-degree relatives with visas when they do not have a sponsor. This visa is for freelancers, some skilled employees, and some investors.

6. Student visa: There are a number of competitive universities in the UAE, just a few of which are New York University and the Sorbonne. The UAE is continuing to grow its reputation as an attractive destination for foreign students, and this visa is offered to anyone studying in the UAE, as long as they have been accepted at a relevant university. There are also some benefits that graduates can tap into after they finish their studies, such as eligibility for the Golden Visa.

7. Retirement visa: These visas are also relatively new, and are offered to people over the age of 55 that can provide evidence that they have the means to sustain themselves without having to work in the UAE.

8. Investor visa: If you are planning on setting up a business or are a major shareholder in a company, you can apply for an investor visa. You can also do this if you have a significant investment in real estate in the country.

For more in-depth information, I would suggest you explore the online platforms for immigration authorities in the UAE: Federal Authority for Identity, Citizenship, Customs & Ports Security (ICP), or General Directorate of Foreign Affairs (GDRFA) in Dubai.

Also, be sure to properly inform yourself of all of the rules about your specific visa, because some of them can be invalidated if you have over a six-month absence away from the UAE. Visa regulations, and rules in general, are taken very seriously here, so it is better to inform yourself and ensure you are following all of the rules.

One new update that was rolled out this year is the Unemployment Insurance Scheme. It is a form of insurance/social security that provides residents working in the federal and private sectors with financial support if they lose their jobs, as a result of termination by their employers. It is mandatory for most people to sign up for it and penalties will be applied for those that do not sign up (luckily it is not very expensive). You should discuss further with your employer to see if you are required to enroll.

Moving your things

Depending on how much stuff you will be bringing to the UAE, you might want to consider hiring an international mover. There are a variety of options for these movers – you can either have them pack your things, or you can do it yourself. You can also have them pick up and drop off everything at your door, or you can collect your belongings from the port directly (this is a more budget-friendly option). You might also want to consider getting insurance, depending on the value of your items (and how much they mean to you).

I would recommend contacting a variety of companies to see what services they offer, and how they can work with your budget. I was originally quoted $5000 for my move from the Netherlands to Dubai and got the price down to $950 (with a little extra work on my end of course). If you are shipping via larger cities or more common routes the pricing will be lower, so see if there are other options available that might help to lower the cost.

Before agreeing to any quote be sure to read the fine print and inform yourself of any extra costs that might be added on at the end of the process. For example, where is the pick-up and drop-off? Will they unpack your belongings and assemble your furniture? Will the company arrange customs and importation documents on your behalf? If so, what other duties or fees could be charged for this? How long do they expect the shipping to take? What are the contact details for any third-party agents that will be dealing with the removal in your destination country?

Also, it is recommended that you take a full inventory of your possessions to be moved, especially if you decide to get insurance (this is normally a requirement for any insurance claims).

There are a number of items which are strictly prohibited from entering the country, so be sure to not bring any of these items or you could run into issues when it is being processed by customs. This includes political or religious literature, firearms or weapons (including toys), alcoholic beverages, narcotics and drugs, items made of ivory or from endangered animals, broadcast transmission and reception sets, counterfeit money, artwork that might be considered erotic, and pork meat and products.

Finally, one personal tip that I learned from my move – assume it will take months for your belongings to arrive, and pack accordingly. My belongings were supposed to take one month to arrive and only arrived four months later, meaning I had to buy an entire new wardrobe for my job. So please make sure that you hand carry any important documents, medicine, or other items that you might need, as you do not want to be stuck without them for weeks (or months in some cases).

Shipping a car

Some people moving to the UAE decide to bring their own car with them, especially when employers offer to pay for the shipment of the vehicle. While this may seem enticing, there are a number of considerations to be aware of.

To begin, there will be a number of fees for insurance and registration, as well as a tax equal to 5% of the vehicle's current valuation. This adds up quickly. You will also need to show a number of documents including registration forms, a certificate of origin and invoice, passports, driver's licenses, insurance, employer's letters and more.

After this, you will also need to conform the car to the specifications for use in the UAE, called GCC specifications, which will mean that the car likely will need renovations before it is considered roadworthy (and before it can be officially registered). These specifications help to prepare the car for the unique environment of the region so will have modifications made to the air filters, radiators, and air conditioners. It will also provide better corrosion and dust protection, so will be better for your car in the long run!

Because of this, many have found that buying a car in the UAE is much cheaper than importing one and requires less paperwork and headache. It is not impossible to import a car, but make sure you understand the requirements before making the decision.

CHAPTER 2

YOUR FIRST DAYS

In your first days on the ground in the UAE, there are a number of things you will need to do to get settled. This will likely include starting to look for an apartment, getting your government documents in order, and hopefully seeing some of the cities themselves.

Arriving at the airport

When you arrive at the airport, you will need to make sure that when you are going through customs you show your initial employment visa (which should be provided by your employer before you depart). If you forget to do this, you can always go back to the airport to register it after, but will be a bit of a hassle. If you are not sponsored by an employer, make sure to read the fine print on your visa to understand if you need to do anything specific upon arrival.

From the airport, you can always go to the taxi stand and they will take you wherever you need to go. All taxis in each Emirate have straightforward pricing that is set by the government, and the drivers are very honest here so you do not have to worry about being taken on circuitous routes. Most also accept credit cards, so it should be quite an easy first ride for you in the country.

Where to stay in your first days

If you are being sponsored by an employer, most of time you will be provided with a hotel for between two weeks and a month after you arrive. If you only have two weeks (as I did), you should make clear backup plans as finding a place to stay within two weeks can be difficult (especially because you need your Emirates ID to secure a place to live, which can take weeks in itself to process).

Luckily, there are a number of good options for intermediate housing, and many hotels will give weekly or monthly discounts. If you are not sure how long you will be staying, or if you prefer to avoid the hassle of renting and furnishing an apartment, there are a number of high-quality furnished apartment hotels that can be a good choice for expatriates (but this convenience normally comes at a higher cost).

With so much to do – where should you start?

My advice is that, in your first day(s), the most important thing to do is to get a phone plan and to start the process to apply for your Emirates ID (which your employer should help with, if you are being sponsored). In order to do this, you will need to get your biometrics taken at your local government entity and you will need a health screening with the Department of Health. Without those, you will not be able to get your Emirates ID, and without that, you will not be able to do much else. After taking those steps, you should focus on finding a place to live and setting up a bank account – everything will fall into place naturally once you have those set in stone.

CHAPTER 3

CHOOSING WHERE TO LIVE

The UAE is comprised of seven "Emirates" (listed in alphabetical order): Abu Dhabi, Ajman, Dubai, Fujairah, Ras Al Khaimah, Sharjah, and Umm Al Quwain. The Emirates in themselves function like states, where there are a number of decisions made at a federal level (such as foreign policy, currency, defense), and some other decisions are made at a state level.

Abu Dhabi and Dubai have the largest number of expatriate residents by far, so we will focus on these Emirates in this book. But that does not mean that the other Emirates do not have great things to offer you – each Emirate has its own "personality", so I would recommend exploring them all.

When it comes to choosing between Abu Dhabi and Dubai, each of the Emirates has vastly different personalities with regards to the "vibe" of the city, and both are undergoing rapid changes. Abu Dhabi is known to be a calmer place, and generally has a reputation for being more family-friendly, whereas Dubai is very energetic and always bustling. Abu Dhabi is also the governmental capital, while Dubai is known as the business hub. From a financial perspective, housing in Abu Dhabi tends to be a bit more expensive, but lifestyle in Dubai is more expensive, so it almost evens out. Luckily, given they are a little over an hour drive away from each other, you can also have the both of the best of both worlds by visiting the other often.

As a side note, it is always worth double checking with your employer if there are any restrictions on where you can live, because sometimes there are certain restrictions based on which organization you are working for. Many families also end up commuting between cities, so it is also not impossible to do that.

Where to live in Abu Dhabi

There are a number of wonderful places to live in Abu Dhabi, these are just a few of the main areas that have the largest expat communities:

- ➢ Reem Island – This is my personal favorite, as it is close to most areas around the city and it has Galleria Mall (which is fantastic). A lot of expats live here which means that many of your new friends might also be your neighbors if you live here, which would be ideal. One downside to Reem is that if you live deep inside of the island, you could add about 15-20 minutes of a commute for yourself because of how many traffic lights there are as you go to the other side of the island. But you are likely to have a better view of the water, so there is a tradeoff. Another possible drawback is that there is always a lot of construction going on since it is developing so quickly, but this is not normally inhibitive (and there are almost no issues with noise). One positive side of this is that there are great new housing options being made available every year. So, it is really not bad.

- Saadiyat Island – Many expats love Saadiyat as it is a beautiful and calm area, and is great for families. There are also some wonderful beaches and the Maamsha al Saadiyat boardwalk, one of my personal favorites. The downside with Saadiyat is that you will need to pay more to live here, as most of the housing comes at a considerably higher pricing point (especially if you are in the Maamsha al Saadiyat area). But if that is not an issue for you – then go for it! You will not be disappointed.

- Yas Island – Yas is known as the "entertainment" hub of Abu Dhabi, with theme parks and water parks galore. It is also a wonderful place to live, especially if you want more space – there are many large villas available in this area.

The downside to Yas is that it is slightly outside of central Abu Dhabi (on the way to Dubai), so you are looking at a 30-40 minute commute if you are working in central Abu Dhabi.

➢ Al Muneera / Al Raha Beach – Al Muneera is another wonderful expat hub slightly outside of central Abu Dhabi. It is located closer to the airport than other places, so could be ideal if you have to travel a lot. It is also very green in the area, and there is less construction than in Reem Island, since most of the area has already been developed. Al Muneera also has a wonderful private beach that select residents of the area get access to (if you are considering living here, check to see if this is included in your rent). One potential downside is that, similar to Yas, you are slightly outside of central Abu Dhabi, so you might have a slightly longer commute depending on where you are working. And similar to Saaidyat, you will normally see higher pricing in this area than in Reem for example (especially if you want beach access). Al Muneera is especially known for being a great place for families, so you might want to consider this if you have children.

Where to live in Dubai

Like Abu Dhabi, Dubai has many wonderful living options, and because it is such a large city, you might want to explore a number of areas to see where you feel most comfortable. These are just a few options:

- ➢ Dubai Marina – As its name implies, Dubai Marina is a 3km marina built around a waterway, offering access to gardens, boats, restaurants, fitness clubs, and health resorts. It is a lively area, and is nice throughout the year. The marina boasts a breathtaking skyline filled with luxurious high-rise apartments and hotels.

- ➢ Business Bay – Business Bay in Dubai is a centrally located, dynamic neighborhood close to iconic landmarks like the Burj Khalifa, offering residents a blend of world-class amenities and a diverse community. While it's an ideal residence for professionals due to its proximity to major businesses, potential residents should be mindful of occasional traffic congestion during peak hours. Overall, its benefits and vibrant atmosphere make it a top choice for those seeking a balanced urban lifestyle in Dubai.

- ➢ Jumeirah Lake Towers (JTL) – Jumeirah Lake Towers mirrors the luxury and scenic waterfront views of Dubai

Marina but offers a more budget-friendly lifestyle. While both communities boast a plethora of amenities, JLT stands out for its affordability without compromising on quality. Additionally, its strategic location provides excellent connectivity to the city, especially with the Dubai Metro running through the area, making it an ideal choice for those prioritizing accessibility and value for money in a vibrant urban setting.

- Al Barsha – Al Barsha is a contemporary residential haven, standing out amidst the city's modern neighborhoods. Its prime location ensures easy accessibility to major city attractions, while offering housing options that are both modern and reasonably priced. The area is characterized by its diverse international community, bringing together cultures from around the world. Residents can enjoy a range of nearby amenities, from shopping malls like Mall of the Emirates to parks and dining options. With its emphasis on safety and family-friendly environment, Al Barsha is an ideal choice for those seeking a balanced lifestyle in Dubai.

- Jumeirah Beach Residence (JBR) – Jumeirah Beach Residence is one of Dubai's premier beachfront communities, offering a blend of cosmopolitan living and coastal relaxation. Comparable to the luxury of Dubai Marina, JBR stands out with its unique beachside location and a pedestrian-friendly promenade brimming with cafes, shops, and entertainment venues. While it boasts upscale amenities and residences, JBR is particularly celebrated for its direct access to the beach, making it a sought-after destination for both residents and tourists. Its strategic position also ensures easy connectivity to key parts of the city, making JBR a harmonious fusion of urban sophistication and beachside charm.

CHAPTER 4

GOVERNMENT DOCUMENTS

One of your biggest priorities after you set foot in the country should be to get your government documentation sorted out – without it, you will not be able to do much else to get yourself settled!

Getting these documents can sometimes take a lot of time and patience, but once you everything is set up, it should be smooth sailing from there. Given that you need an Emirates ID to get open a bank account and to rent an apartment, you will find that you may be blocked from finalizing some of your other activities until this is done – but that does not mean you cannot make progress on them in parallel. Sometimes if you explain to a bank or housing company that you are waiting for your ID to arrive to come in, they will let you tentatively proceed in starting to set things up. This way all you will have to do once you get the ID is to share a scan with them so they can finalize everything.

One of my favorite things about living here is how digitalized the government is, almost everything you need to do can be done via an app, and I love having an application on my phone that stores the digital versions of my identity card and my driver's license on it. So once you have everything in sorted out, it should be very easy after that.

Emirates ID

The UAE Resident Identity Card is often called an "Emirates ID" or an "EID" for short – it is issued by the Federal Authority for Identity, Citizenship, Customs and Ports Security. It is legally required that UAE citizens and residents apply for one and carry it with them at all times.

The Emirates ID is not just an ID, but will be your portal to a number of government and non-government services when you are living here. For example, it is used for opening bank accounts, applying for a driver's license, renewing your vehicle registration,

Sample Emirates ID

connecting utilities, renting properties, and applying for insurance.

To apply for the Emirates ID, you will need to follow a number of steps (sometimes the steps may differ slightly depending on which visa you have):

1. Register yourself online through the ICP website (you can even do this before you arrive)
2. Go to an accredited typing center with an ICP section (you will also be asked to provide your passport and entry permit information at this stage)
3. Pay the service and card fee, which varies depending on the visa you are applying for, and how long you are staying (a normal range is Dh170 up to Dh1,070+ for the Golden Visa)
4. Visit an ICP Center for your biometric scan
5. When the ID is ready, the post office will send you a message to collect your Emirates ID from the branch mentioned in your application, or you can pay to have it delivered

Your Emirates ID can sometimes take a number of weeks, so try to be as patient as possible on this. But as mentioned, make sure this is a priority for you from day one. As you are waiting to receive the physical card, the

ICA UAE Phone Application

Federal Authority for Identity and Citizenship will likely issue you with an e-version for use in the interim. To access this, you can download the ICA UAE Smart app (as pictured). You can then register your details and access your e-Emirates ID card (as soon as it is ready).

If you are being sponsored by an employer, they should help you with registering for the Emirates ID. This will be a big relief for those who do have assistance in the process!

In general, you will need a state-administered medical exam (you cannot get it before you come or from a private doctor – this is discussed further in Chapter 12), and to register your biometrics. When you have done both of these, you will need to officially apply for the residency visa, and to pay the fees that are associated with all of those.

Driver's license

You cannot apply for a driver's license before you have your Emirates ID, so be patient and realize that it is going to take some time (it took me two months, just as a frame of reference).

Depending on which country you are from, there are different processes to follow. Check on the Ministry of Interior website (the Markhoos service), or on the RTA website, to learn more about whether you will be able to convert your home license into a UAE driving license. Also check the Abu Dhabi and Dubai government websites before you go to the center, as the rules and requirements sometimes change.

Sample driver's license

> **If you are from a country that has dual recognition of driving licenses with the UAE,** you will need to bring your former license (that is at least one year old), your original passport, your original Emirates ID, passport-size photographs (they normally have a booth in the offices if you need it), a recent eye test (this can be done at the offices too), and a No Objection Certificate from your sponsor or employer (only in specific

At the time of writing, the following countries have driver's license recognition with the UAE:
GCC Countries, Australia, Austria, Belgium, Canada, Denmark, Finland, France, Germany, Greece, Ireland, Italy, Japan, Netherlands, New Zealand, Norway, Poland, Portugal, Romania, South Africa, Spain, South Korean, Sweden, Switzerland, Turkey, UK, USA

situations is this required). You will also need to pay to have the license professionally translated. Total, I paid less than Dh800 for the entire conversion process, so you can expect something in this realm (also make sure to bring cash). If all goes well and if you arrive early enough in the day, you can normally pick up your license on the same day (for this reason I recommend going in the morning – it will take a few hours).

- ➢ **If you are from a country that does not have dual recognition of driving licenses with the UAE**, you will need to register for a course and take an exam before being able to get your driver's license. You must take the necessary training courses and attend all required lectures for a period of 8 hours each, before being permitted to begin the practical driving classes. Make sure you attend the theoretical courses at an authorized driving school, otherwise it will not be recognized. The cost for this process normally ranges between Dh4500 and Dh7000.

I should also note that there is a law that you cannot rent a car without having a UAE driver's license if you are a resident (even if you have your home license or an international driver's license), which means often that many expats cannot drive in their first few weeks here. Luckily taxis are very easy (and cheap) to use so it is not that difficult to navigate around in the first few weeks. But, if you plan on driving, it is worth trying to get this handled as quickly as possible.

Also, like with the Emirates ID, you can download an app that stores your digital driver's license. If you live in Abu Dhabi, this used to be the Abu Dhabi Police application, which also stored your car registration and kept track of any driving fines or infractions that you have. This has recently changed to Tamm so I would recommend downloading both to be safe. These apps are a must-have if you are in the Emirate. If you live in Dubai, you can down application, where you can also log mino event that they happen.

UAE Pass

UAE Pass is a digital identification application for your phone, that can be used to authenticate various smart services in the country, digitally sign, request, and verify documents. You will need to have your Emirates ID to register on the application, so put this on the backburner until that is handled (I only use mine a few times a year so it is not immediately crucial, but you will normally need it to rent an apartment).

CHAPTER 5

BANKING

There are a number of great banks in the UAE, so while you should put some thought into which bank you go with, it is hard to go wrong. My advice is to see which banks are offering the best deals at the moment (normally this is listed on their websites) and you can choose the bank that offers the most benefits.

Bank options

There are four types of banks in the UAE: commercial, industrial, merchant, and Islamic. You can use any of them, so do not worry too much about the type of bank. Most expats I know in Abu Dhabi will either use the First Abu Dhabi bank (known as FAB), or Abu Dhabi Commercial Bank (known as ADCB). For those in Dubai, Emirates National Bank of Dubai

(ENBD) is also a great option. Some international banks also have operations in the UAE, including CitiBank, HSBC, Royal Bank of Canada, and UBS.

If you earn a monthly income of over Dh50,000 (normally) you can also be invited to an "Elite" program at most of the banks, where you will have a private banker to provide you with more personalized assistance. In my experience, it does not provide that much of a benefit, but it does not hurt to have (especially since it is free).

You will need to have your Emirates ID before you can open a bank account in the UAE. You will also be asked for other documentation, such as your passport and (possibly) a letter from your employer. You will also need a letter which provides proof of your salary if you want to join any of the Elite programs. Since you will not be able to get paid without a local bank account, you might want to open an international bank account before you go (make sure it has a branch in the UAE and that your account is in AED), just so you are not stranded without access to money.

My final suggestion on banks is to always check what benefits you can get to open a new account, if you are getting one anyways you might as well see what kind of perks you can get from it!

Transfers

At some points, most expats will need to transfer money home. Transfer costs can add up easily here, so it is worth putting time into understanding how you can keep the costs as low for yourself as possible.

There are a few primary ways that expats transfer money home:

1. You can send a transfer in AED to your home account (in your home currency) via your local bank in the UAE. Many banks will give you one free transfer per month in this situation, but the transfer rate is not guaranteed (and your home bank might take extra fees out to receive the money).

2. You can take out an account in your home currency in the UAE, and transfer money from your home currency in the UAE to your home bank. For example, I have a friend from Belgium who took out a Euro account at ADCB – every month he changes his AED income to EUR within the UAE and then he will send a Euro-to-Euro transfer to his Belgium bank account. He does need to pay a transfer fee when he exchanges the AED to EUR, but then he can choose when he does the exchange based on when the rates are most beneficial.

3. You can use a third-party service such as Western Union or Wise to send money home – there are also fees involved

in these options, and from my research they tend to be a bit more expensive than the first two options.

Also ask your bank what transfer benefits they provide, as often you can get one free international transfer per month.

No matter what, there will be fees involved in transfers, it is just the price you pay. It is always better than having to pay income taxes ☺!

CHAPTER 6

PHONE PLANS

When it comes to phone plans, there are three main companies that you can choose from: Du, Etisalat, and Virgin Mobile. There is not a major difference in the coverage itself (coverage is great everywhere in the UAE), but there are considerable differences in the pricing.

One very important point to keep in mind, and something that you should check before you leave, is whether your phone is locked. If your phone is locked you will need to pay your carrier from your home country to unlock it, otherwise you will not be able to use a UAE SIM card in your phone.

After you arrive, I would suggest getting a pre-paid SIM, which should hold you over for the first month (you can get a tourist package that lasts from 30-90 days). You can even get these at one of the airport kiosks when you arrive.

While you can pay as you go at the beginning, you should definitely look for good deals at all three of these companies, as I have saved thousands of Dirhams in a year by changing phone plans. One example, is that Virgin Mobile will give you a 50% discount if you pay for the entire year up front. It also has an easy-to-use application that allows users to scale their plans up or down based on their usage, and if they travel abroad, they can easily add on minutes or data roaming for that country so that they do not have to worry about getting a SIM card when they arrive. It is also a requirement that once you have your Emirates ID that you change to a "resident SIM," so keep it in mind that you will probably have to do this in your second or third month in the country.

Most phone plans here will include some mixture of three items: local minutes, international minutes, and data. The international minutes are especially helpful if you need to stay in touch with family or friends back home, as many in-app audio/video capabilities do not work in the country (this includes WhatsApp, FaceTime, Skype, etc.).

CHAPTER 7

SEARCHING FOR A PLACE TO LIVE

For many people, one of the biggest headaches of moving here is trying to find a place to live. The markets move very quickly, so even if you find the place of your dreams, you might try to make a down payment on it just to find out that it has already been taken by someone else. So make sure that you are prompt in your follow-up and that you move quickly if you find a place you love.

Prices

The biggest expense most expats will have in the UAE is accommodation. Although housing in both Abu Dhabi and Dubai are easy to come by and there is a large range of prices and options, you will need to pay more to find a nice place (as with all cities).

In general, rental rates will depend on the location and size of the property to be rented. For example, prices will be slightly higher in Abu Dhabi than in Dubai, and there are also slightly fewer options in Abu Dhabi (though they are expanding rapidly). The average rent in Dubai can still be anywhere between Dhs60,000 and Dhs180,000 per year, but you can easily go above that, especially if you have a villa (there are also options below that). The average rent in Abu Dhabi could be anywhere between Dhs80,000 (for a one bedroom) to Dhs200,000 (for a three bedroom) per year, but you can also go above or below that of course.

There is also higher turnover in the markets here because everyone wants to live in new buildings, so something will be considered "older" even if it is more than five years old (pushing the prices up even further on newer places).

Finding a place

To find available places for rent or for sale, you can search for available accommodations using local newspapers, registered real estate brokers (agents), or private property websites. You can also find properties rented directly from the owner on these sites.

Some of the best websites to use are:

- Property Finder
- MyBayut
- Dubizzle
- Facebook groups also have a lot of great finds (be careful of scammers here)

My advice is to try to do as much as possible yourself through the websites, because agents fees get very expensive very quickly (I had to pay 5% of my annual rental as a fee, and they only did a few hours of work in helping me). Sometimes there is no way around paying agent fees, or sometimes they are already included in the apartment price, so you will just need to see how flexible you are willing to be (and how much you actually want the place!).

When you are negotiating your contract, it is also a good idea to ask if you can either get a 13th month for free (i.e. 13 months of rent for the price of 12) or if you might secure a discount if you pay for everything up front (which is especially useful if your company is helping you). Also be sure to ask whether the place you are renting comes with appliances included (normally they do not).

On your search, you will quickly find that most apartments in the UAE are very modern, spacious, and well-designed, and that complexes tend to include other facilities like gyms, pools, and parking at no extra charge.

Rental contracts

To begin, most rental contracts are for at least a year, and it is very common that you are asked to pay in advance via "cheques" (normally which are all requested ahead of time, and then are cashed either quarterly, biannually, or yearly). If you want to leave your contract early you probably will not be granted a refund, but sometimes exceptions are made to this rule. A deposit will also be requested, which will be between 5% and 10% of the annual price.

One nice thing about renting here is that landlords in certain areas are also forbidden from raising rent prices more than a certain percentage every year, and housing is regulated quite closely in general (if you ever have any rental disputes, you can contact the Rent Dispute Settlement Committee in Abu Dhabi or the Real Estate Legislation team in Dubai).

In the UAE, it is not uncommon for banks to manage properties, which is sometimes helpful as they work with pretty good management companies.

Once you have found a place to rent, you will need to provide the agency with documentation which normally includes a copy of your Emirates ID, a passport, a valid residency visa, and a few other things (sometimes a letter from your employer as well). You will also need your housing contract to be registered with the local governing body, which is done through the UAE Pass application.

Registering your rental

Lease agreements between landlords and tenants must be registered with the respective authority in each Emirate (this is a legal requirement). Registration of the contracts is required in order to connect the utility services (including water, electricity, gas, phone, and internet), so there is no way around this.

In Abu Dhabi, landlords have to register lease contracts in the Tawtheeq system, which is the city's register for tenancy contracts. Once the lease contract has been registered, a housing fee of a certain percent of the total value of the annual rent will be taken across the rental period (sometimes in different proportions each month). This amount will be added to the monthly water and electricity bill of the tenant. To register the contract, the landlord or manager will send a digital document to the UAE Pass application for you to sign, and once you approve, the contract will be officially recorded under your name and Emirates ID.

In Dubai, the system is similar, but landlords must register lease agreements with the online portal Ejari. Tenants will pay housing fees to Dubai Municipality, which is a certain percent of the annual rental charges. And similar to Abu Dhabi, the housing fees are added to the monthly electricity and water bills.

Buying property

Buying in the UAE is a bit different than buying in other countries so my recommendation is to rent when you first arrive, just so you have time to get your feet on the ground and understand how everything works. Even if rental prices seem high, buying is normally only a good option if you are planning on staying more than five years (or in investing for at least that amount of time). Most expats you meet will choose to rent, especially because there is normally a high down payment requested on houses, in addition to a bevy of fees and commissions (which add up quickly).

If you are planning on investing in the country or need to secure a visa through investment, you might also consider buying property to gain access to some of the special visa programs that the country offers (normally this requires a significant investment).

If you do decide to buy, you will need to decide whether you want a leasehold property or a freehold property. A leasehold will essentially be a very long-term rental property, which you would lose access to after a set amount of time. A freehold, which is only available in certain areas of the country (which continue to expand every year) will be completely owned by you.

Similarly to renting, you will normally need an agent if you decide to buy, and there will be a fee for this as well (along with a few other fees). If you need a mortgage for your purchase, you normally will need at least 25% cash down plus the associated purchase costs, according to the UAE mortgage law, and this number will normally go up if you are buying a second or third property. Also be sure to ask what the annual service charges are for whatever units you are buying - these are recurring fees that homeowners pay for maintenance and upkeep of residential buildings or communities.

CHAPTER 8

UTILITIES AND BILLS

Once you have your rental contract registered, you can start setting up your utilities. Most Emirates have their own utility companies, and everywhere will differ slightly, but normally your monthly utilities should be grouped as follows:

1. Electricity/Water/Sewage/Municipality Housing Fee
2. Gas (if applicable to your apartment)
3. Air conditioning (again, if applicable to your apartment – sometimes it is included in your rent)
4. Internet & cable

This is meant as a guideline of what to be aware of so it could differ based on where you are living. It is also important to note that all utility set-up will require you to provide your Emirates ID or passport, and your tenancy agreement.

Utilities in Abu Dhabi

1. Electricity/Water/Sewage/Municipality Housing Fee: This will be run by the Abu Dhabi Distribution Company (ADDC) and should be set up automatically when you register your housing contract through the Tawtheeq program. It has an online payment system and is very straightforward to use. Make sure to inform them when you are leaving so they can prepare your final bill and you can receive your security deposit back (many people forget to do this).

2. Gas (if applicable to your apartment): These systems can differ slightly so you will need to follow the instructions provided to you by your building management team, the most common company in Abu Dhabi is SERGAS.

3. Air conditioning (again, if applicable to your apartment): If you have centralized air conditioning there is a chance your air conditioning will not be included (always ask before you decide to rent, as the summer months can get expensive).

4. Internet (unless you pay for a year up front): Etisalat used to be the main provider but Virgin and Du have emerged as great options too. Virgin will give you 50% off of you pay for a year up front (but you will also need to buy your

own router, which is an additional expense you should calculate in). Ask what promotions these companies have when you are signing up as you can usually get a month or two for free.

Utilities in Dubai

1. Electricity/Water/Sewage/Municipality Housing Fee: In Dubai, you will need to set up an account with the Dubai Electricity and Water Authority (DEWA). You can sign up online, and you will need to pay activation fees and a security deposit, and everything should be up and running in less than 24 hours. Make sure you inform them before you leave so that you can deactivate your service and recollect your security deposit (many people forget to do this).

2. Gas (if applicable to your apartment): These systems can differ slightly so you will need to follow the instructions provided to you by your building management team, the most common company in Dubai is Emirates Gas.

3. Air conditioning (again, if applicable to your apartment): If you have centralized air conditioning there is a chance your air conditioning will not be included (always ask

before you decide to rent, as the summer months can get expensive).

4. Internet: Etisalat used to be the main provider but Virgin and Du have emerged as great options too. Virgin will give you 50% off of you pay for a year up front (but you will also need to buy your own router, which is an additional expense you should calculate in). Ask what promotions these companies have when you are signing up as you can usually get a month or two for free.

Recycling

If you are interested, be sure to ask your building management team or neighbors about recycling. It was not that common here a few years ago but it has become much more popular in recent years. For example, I am signed up to a plastic recycling program called Recapp, which will come to collect my plastic every few weeks (when I have two full bags). It is run entirely by app and is completely free, and the more you recycle the more you get points, which can be used for different benefits around the country.

CHAPTER 9

GETTING AROUND

Learning to get around will be very important for you in your first weeks in the country, and luckily it is easy to do. Public transport is improving every year, and Dubai has a wonderful metro system. The UAE is also launching a national rail network, called Etihad Rail, which is currently under construction and should be ready for passenger use soon. That being said, cars and taxis are still the most popular ways to get around the cities, so do not rule out any options until you get here.

Car

Emiratis and expats alike are known for their love of driving and many people have cars here. For those that are not sure how long they will be staying or are hesitant to buy in general, there are long-term rental options available at most major car rental agencies.

Buying a car

Before you buy a car, you will want to check to see if it has had any accidents or if there are any other fees attached to the car. You can do this in a number of ways but I would recommend using the Emirates Vehicle Gate website, where you can run a check using the vehicle's chassis/VIN number. Every accident that has taken place in the country should be on there. It sometimes happens that people are not given the full or accurate vehicle histories before they purchase a car, so I would make sure to do your due diligence if you want to buy a used vehicle (and also get a full vehicle inspection done before finalizing any deal). My recommendation is to buy new cars from the dealerships, if possible, as you will be 100% certain with what you are getting that way.

If you are going to buy a car from a dealer or agency, normally you can ask them to help arrange the car registration (called "Mulkiya" – which needs to be renewed every year). For this, you will need to provide your UAE residency visa, passport, Emirates ID, a valid UAE driving license, and proof of insurance (you will need to get insurance before the car is registered, it normally costs 1-3% of the car's value). You can contact many insurance companies and see who has the best offer and who will give you the most benefits. Sometimes you can also ask for a complimentary/discounted "Orange Card," which is free insurance for Oman, in case you want to drive across the border. If you want to drive to other countries in the Gulf you will need to make sure you have the proper insurance in place before doing so (sometimes you can also buy it at the border).

There are two main types of insurance:

- Third-party Liability Insurance – this is the minimum amount of insurance required by law and will protect you from claims you are liable for including injury, loss of life, or damage to vehicles and property. The policy does not cover your car repair costs or medical care.

- Comprehensive Coverage – this is more expensive but will cover you from both third-party claims and damage to your own vehicle, which often (but not always) includes fire, burglary, vandalism, and theft as well.

When comparing options, one of the main things to be aware of is whether you want agency repairs (i.e., by the dealer) or if you are fine having your car repaired anywhere. You might also want to look for roadside assistance, personal effects coverage, a replacement rental car, or off-road coverage, depending on what your needs are. You can also request a "No

Claims Bonus" if you have not had an accident in the previous year.

It is important to note that if your car is damaged in any way (even if you accidentally damage it yourself), you will need to file a police report, as repair companies cannot repair damaged cars without a relevant police report being filed.

Also, if you decide to buy a used car, make sure it is not for "re-export only" as you will not be able to use it in the UAE without paying a number of additional taxes and fees.

One final fun fact to think about when you are purchasing your car is that license plates are a matter of prestige here. If you have a nice pattern (e.g. 12345) or it matches the final digits of your phone number, people will likely comment on it. The best license plates are auctioned off for hundreds of thousands of AED.

Road safety

When driving, if you have an accident, you will always need to file a police report (call 999 for emergency services), and without this report you cannot file an insurance claim. Also take pictures of your car, just in case they are necessary down the road (this should also be done for the police report). The police often will decide at the accident site who is "at fault" for the accident, which makes insurance claims processing pretty straightforward and fast.

Tolls

If you buy a car, make sure to register it with the relevant Emirate's automated toll gates as there are not physical toll booths and you could be subject to a fine if you drive through them without registering (and therefore without paying).

For Abu Dhabi you will need to register with the Darb toll gate system, which will charge you if you drive through the gates during peak hours (it is not very expensive). I prepay in bulk a few times a year so I do not have to think about it. It is a very high-tech system in that once you pass through any of them, your vehicle is identified through its plate number; then a specified fee is deducted from your account's wallet. Right now, the morning peak timing is 7-9 am and the evening peak timing is 5-7 pm.

For Dubai, the process is slightly different as you will need to buy a Salik tag at any participating gas station or store, and then you will need to create an account before using it. The tag will need to be put on your windshield in order for it to be properly registered when you use it. I would recommend registering with both when you arrive as you will likely travel through both cities so will need both tolls at some point.

Parking

As with many services in the country, parking is done primarily by app here. There are a number of parking apps, but Mawaqif is good because you can use it across all of the Emirates. You can also pay via text but it is very complex and took a while for me to figure out how to do it properly, so my advice is to use an app and save yourself the headache!

Driving rules

While the UAE is a very open and tolerant country, it enforces its laws very seriously, and I highly recommend that everyone reading this take care not to break any laws (on the roads or elsewhere). The penalties are more severe than in many Western countries so it would behoove you to be careful.

To begin, the UAE has a zero-tolerance policy for drunk driving - even one drink before driving might get you a prison sentence of up to six months and fines of between Dhs5,000 and Dhs20,000.

As mentioned before, you must also immediately report road and traffic accidents to the police in the UAE. If anything happens, you should call the police on 999 (from anywhere in the UAE), give them your location, and wait for their instructions. On the other hand, you can report a minor accident in Dubai via the Dubai Police mobile application. Driving through red lights is also taken very seriously, and be cautious not to talk on the phone or text, as this will equally get you into trouble.

When it comes to speeding, tickets can go above Dhs15,000 (though this is not common), so again, be careful and ensure you are following the rules at all times. There is an unwritten rule that you can go up to 20 km/h over the limit in Dubai but that in Abu Dhabi you might get a ticket even if you are only 1 km/h over the speed limit. There are many speed traps in the country, so do not think you will be able to get around them for long. My advice is to stay under the limit everywhere and then you won't have a problem!

If you are caught breaking the rules, you should be aware that "points" will be deducted from your license except for minor infringements. You have 24 points in one year before you lose your license – so be careful (drunk driving for example will make you lose all 24 points immediately).

Taxis

For people that do not want to drive, taxis in the Emirates can be a great alternative. They are highly visible in cities and very affordable, and they are regulated heavily which leads to a pretty good experience for passengers (taxis are closely monitored so they should never take circuitous routes). Most taxi drivers also speak English very well, and in Dubai they even have a "Ladies Only" taxi option.

Aside from taxis, you can also take Uber and Careem in the UAE. Uber tends to be slightly more expensive than taxis and Careem is probably the most affordable option of the three (but has less coverage in Abu Dhabi).

As a final note, do not accept any rides from non-licensed drivers offering you a lift in exchange for money. This is illegal and you can get in trouble for doing so.

Public transport

There is an expansive network of buses throughout Abu Dhabi and Dubai, that are highly efficient, affordable, and clean. You may find all routes and timings on the Darb app in Abu Dhabi (which only has buses) and on the RTA app in Dubai (which has buses and a metro - there is even a Ladies Only section on the Dubai Metro).

You can also take buses between cities, which is a very affordable option if you are looking to go from Dubai to Abu Dhabi or visa versa. A bus ticket may cost around Dhs40 while a taxi could cost Dhs300 (or more). To do this, you would need to go to the Central Bus Station in each Emirate, which will normally be equipped with restrooms, prayer rooms (for Muslims), and cafes.

CHAPTER 10

LOCAL CUSTOMS AND CULTURE

The UAE is a Muslim country, which you will see deeply intertwined in many parts of your life here. It is also an incredibly tolerant and open country that welcomes people from many faiths and cultural backgrounds - and the fact that it is a melting pot of cultures and people is one of my favorite things about the country. While it is a melting pot, it is also a good idea to educate yourself about Islam before you arrive, as it will add a lot of depth to your experience here (and may also save you from some unintended cultural faux pas!).

Safety

Another thing I like about living here is that the UAE is incredibly safe (and was rated the safest place in the world for women to live in 2021). It is a relief not having to worry where I am walking or at what hour, and I have never heard of anything being stolen in the country while I have been here. Once you arrive you will hear some variation of a joke that you can leave your phone on a table and come back months later, and it will still be there.

Public holidays

There are nine public holidays in the UAE, though the dates for some of these change year by year.

These include (for 2023):

- 1 January (Sunday): New Year's Day
- 20–23 April (Thursday through Sunday): Eid al-Fitr holiday
- 27 June (Tuesday): Arafat (Hajj) Day
- 28–30 June (Wednesday through Friday): Eid al-Adha (Feast of Sacrifice)
- 19 July (Wednesday): Al-Hijra (Islamic New Year)
- 1 December (Friday): Commemoration Day
- 2–3 December (Saturday to Sunday): National Day

And the following public holidays are expected in 2024, but the exact dates may still change:

- 1 January (Monday): New Year's Day
- 8–10 April (Monday through Wednesday): Eid al-Fitr
- 15 June (Saturday): Arafat (Hajj) Day
- 16-18 June (Sunday through Tuesday): Eid al-Adha (Feast of Sacrifice)
- 8 July (Monday): Al-Hijra (Islamic New Year)
- 1 December (Sunday): Commemoration Day
- 2–3 December (Monday to Tuesday): National Day

It is important to note that, because Muslim festivals are timed according to local sightings of various phases of the moon, the dates and timings of Islamic holidays can change up until just a few days before the holiday is expected to happen. So make sure you account for last minute changes in your holiday planning if you want to travel during these dates.

Local culture

You may have to get used to certain aspects of the culture, but it should not be a huge adjustment.

Emiratis are very respectful, hospitable, and conservative (though this varies), and the culture in itself is nonconfrontational. Because it is not a very direct culture, you sometimes have to read between the lines if you are not used to this style of communication style. It is also built on social relations so, unlike many Westerners, Emiratis do not like to jump into the main point in meetings, but rather prefer to have some social back and forth first.

In this light, it is also not culturally appropriate to lose your temper in public or to insult people, so you will want to be cautious about this. Gossiping and swearing are also not tolerated, nor are public displays of affection. Public intoxication is also very discouraged and can get you into trouble. Also be cognizant of what you are wearing as it is frowned upon to wear revealing clothing (though you will still see it).

Finally, you will also hear the term "Emirati hospitality" over and over - this is because the UAE has a culture of being generous hosts. This also means that it is impolite to refuse an invitation to a host's home, so if you do not want to accept an invitation it is better to be evasive or vague about meeting up rather than saying "no" outright. If you do attend an event in someone's home, you will likely be segregated by gender, as the men and women will be in different rooms.

Being a woman in the UAE

The UAE ranks first in the world for being a safe place for women. Street harassment is virtually non-existent, and no matter where you are, or at what time of day, you will generally feel very safe, respected, and protected as a woman.

Contrary to many people's stereotypes about the Middle East, women in the country have many rights. For example, women can vote, drive, own property, work, and get an education – and there are even more women than men working in the UAE public sector.

Furthermore, pregnant women are guaranteed paid maternity leave, which is a game changer for many people in the country.

CHAPTER 11

MOVING WITH YOUR FAMILY

Bringing a family to the UAE comes with an entirely different set of considerations, but luckily, this is a very family-friendly country so you should be pleasantly surprised by how smoothly the transition goes. The fact that English is spoken so widely in the country will help too.

Families are highly valued in the UAE, so there are many activities here for children of all ages. This is also an opportunity for you to build your network by speaking to fellow parents at work, or at your children's schools.

In terms of education itself, you will find many options, so there will definitely be something that will fit the needs of both you and your child. Plus, they will get to learn about a new culture, which will help to expand their horizons!

Pregnancy and birth

It can sometimes be difficult to find nice and affordable maternity and breastfeeding clothes (and bras) – so forwarding services like ShopAndShip are a great option if you want something specific, as you can order whatever you need from abroad.

Maternity care in itself is generally very good, though because medical staff come from all over the world, there can sometimes be cultural differences in the treatment. Therefore, when you are looking for a maternity provider, you should consider:

- Do you like them and feel comfortable with them?
- Does your insurance cover them?
- Which hospitals do they deliver at and what facilities does the hospital have (NICU, water birth, etc.)?

It is also important to be aware that some add-on services may not be provided by UAE insurance providers (like NIPT testing), so it is worth discussing this with your insurance provider early on in your pregnancy.

There are also many Facebook Groups and WhatsApp chats for parents living in your area, so be sure to tap into the wealth of advice on these! It may also be a great way to meet fellow parents with children that are a similar age.

In case you do need additional support, you will be able to find doulas, maternity nurses, night nannies, and lactation consultants, so you should always have access to the support you need. Some hospitals will even provide antenatal classes, and if they do not, you can find private classes or hypnobirthing and baby first aid classes.

Fertility treatment and IVF are very common in the UAE and there are many excellent providers, along with fertility doulas who can support you in the process. Some treatments are not permitted in the country, such as egg/sperm donation, surrogacy, and sex selection. It is also important to note that termination of pregnancy is allowed in very limited circumstances. And finally, insurance normally only covers married women, so you should be aware that there will be additional expenses for both the pregnancy and the birth if you are not married.

Childcare

There are a number of great childcare options available in all cities, so you will need to visit them to see which option you feel most comfortable with. The costs will also vary widely depending on the facility, so make sure that you have properly informed yourself before paying any registration fees – costs can range from Dhs10,000-50,000.

In the UAE, children must start compulsory education at age six, but there are a number of preschools, nurseries, and daycares that they can attend before this. In order to access childcare in the UAE, you will need to provide the child's birth certificate, the child and parents' UAE visa, and the child's proof of vaccinations. Many of the private childcare centers will have long waitlists, so ensure that you apply early.

If you would like a nanny, you can hire them individually or through agencies, at a range of costs. If you hire one privately, you will need to sponsor them, and there will be a bit of bureaucracy involved to do so, but they will be relatively cheaper than if you do it through an agency.

Some employers will also offer childcare as a benefit for their employees, so be sure to check on this before signing up for anything.

Schools

For schools, most English-speaking schools in the UAE are private or international schools (expat children are not allowed to attend public schools). Many employers will also subsidize them, so you should see if this is an option available to you (daycares are normally not subsidized). You can find many different curricula, such as the British national curriculum, the International Baccalaureate and American syllabi, among others. Enrollment policies will vary, but your child might be asked to take a test to ensure they are a fit for the courses being taught. So make sure to do your research thoroughly and ask the schools directly if you have any questions.

Also, similar to childcare centers, there are very long waiting lists at schools, so make sure you sign your kids up as early as possible.

Other tips for those with children

- Some of the most well-known baby/child shops are: Mamas & Papas, Mumzworld (online only), First Cry, and Mothercare. You should be able to find what you need at many different pricing points with these options.

- KIDDOS Toy Club is great for people who are looking to avoid child clutter - it is a UAE-based subscription service that will deliver age-appropriate toys to your house every month (at the time of writing it costs Dhs80 per month).

Moving with pets

Moving with pets is honestly a bit of a hassle, so it will require some patience throughout the process. Pets are also culturally taboo, so you will not see a lot of Emiratis with them.

To begin, you will need to get a lot of paperwork done in your home country before you leave for the UAE. You will also need to make sure that your breed of pet is permitted in the country (e.g. "fighting dogs" are not permitted).

In general, the documentation you will need to bring cats and dogs into the country include: a health certificate from your home country veterinarian, vaccination records (including rabies shot within 1 year but at least 30 days before travel), a microchip, and a copy of your passport. Animals under three months of age will not be permitted either.

Be sure to check the UAE Ministry of Environment and Water (MOEW) for the most up to date information on what is or is not required when importing animals.

CHAPTER 12

HEALTH

I have used medical systems in many countries around the world and continue to be impressed by the healthcare I receive in the UAE. The UAE's healthcare system and health insurance are of very high quality and are also incredibly comprehensive with regard to coverage (to live in the country you <u>must</u> have insurance coverage).

When you first arrive

When you first arrive in the country, you will need to get a health screening via a Department of Health approved center. This is normal and everyone has to do it – in essence they will include a general check-up, blood test, and a chest X-ray. These tests screen you for a range of diseases, such as HIV/AIDS, tuberculosis, syphilis, and Hepatitis B. It is likely that when you try to renew your visa you will also need to go through the process again, but you should check what the rules are when you are getting ready to renew as they may change.

Registering your insurance

If you are provided with insurance coverage through your employer, you will need to ask them for the name of the insurance company they use, and normally they can provide a code or coverage information that you can use to access your account (normally your employer should register you when you start working there).

Using your insurance

Insurance is very easy to use in the country, normally you will need to go on the app of your insurance company to find a doctor or a hospital that is in their network, and you can book an appointment with them from there. I would also recommend asking around to see which doctors or hospitals your friends and colleagues use, as you can normally get great tips that way (I always look up reviews on Google as well).

Also, if you know that you will need to see a specialist, try to book an appointment as early as possible as there are sometimes long waiting lists to get into see them (sometimes you will need a referral – check with your insurance company if you have any questions on this).

You will almost always need to pay a small co-pay (depending on your insurance) it is normally very minor – I paid about Dhs50 for an entire emergency room visit once.

Medical tourism

The UAE is also becoming a hub for medical tourism, which is not surprising because it has so many talented doctors and specialists from around the world. If you are considering this, I would highly recommend it – just make sure you do your research to ensure you are getting the right doctor for your needs.

CHAPTER 13

TIPS AND TRICKS

In addition to the content we have covered in previous sections, I wanted to provide you with some suggestions for helpful applications, and a question and answer section, for topics that did not fit into any of the topics I have already discussed.

Recommended phone applications/websites:

General UAE:

- Amazon - online shopping, it has almost everything
- Careem - taxis, food delivery, etc., it is used more in Dubai than in Abu Dhabi
- Carrefour - grocery delivery, it also has a "1 hour delivery" option for certain foods

- Deliveroo - food delivery service
- Dubizzle - website to buy almost anything second-hand
- Entertainer - discount app for restaurants and entertainment
- InstaShop - grocery delivery (but they also have an online pharmacy etc.)
- Justlife - provides a series of at home services, including personal training, cleaning, salon services, maintenance, laundry, pest control, and car washing
- Kibsons - grocery delivery, I have always been impressed by the freshness and quality of their produce
- Mr Usta - repair app, they will connect you to different types of repair people
- Namshi/Noon - online shopping, like Amazon, they have almost everything
- Tier - electric scooter app
- TimeOut - covers events and activities that are going on in both Abu Dhabi and Dubai
- Uber - taxi app
- Udrive - on-demand car rentals for short distances
- Waze - traffic and map app, good for seeing where speed cameras are and finding ways around traffic jams

Abu Dhabi specific applications:

- Abu Dhabi Police - necessary mainly if you have a car, this will hold your license and car registration (and is in the process of being transferred to Tamm, so download both to be safe)
- Abu Dhabi Taxi - local taxi app

Dubai specific applications:

- Cafu - on demand fuel, you log your location and they will fill up your gas tank for you
- HeyChef - a private chef will come to your house to cook for you and your guests
- S'hail - public transportation map for Dubai, will also provide route details and information on estimated fares
- Smart taxi - local taxi app
- Zofeur - an on-demand chauffer service which will take your car wherever you need, whether it is to fill up with petrol, or to drop off dry-cleaning

Commonly asked questions and answers:

Do I need to learn Arabic?

If you learn at least a few words in Arabic, you will likely find it easier to bond with locals, and with Arabic speaking colleagues. It will also show that you respect the place and its people. At the same time, because English is spoken by almost everyone in the country, you will be just fine without it.

How much should I tip?

Given the lower wages of much of the service sector, I tip very often and would encourage others to as well. At restaurants anywhere between 10-15% is the norm, but anything will be appreciated (I always try to tip higher than this).

How do post offices work?

The UAE's postal system is a work in progress, and it will be close to impossible to have letters sent to your home in the country. If you will need to receive mail, I would highly encourage you to set up a PO Box at your local Emirates Post Office. You can also try asking your work if you can use theirs (which a lot of people do), but this is not an option for everyone. If you need packages, you can consider using a shipping forwarding service – I use one called "ShopAndShip" that I would recommend. In essence, they will give you "addresses" around the world, and then you can have any package sent to any of those addresses, and they will forward it to you in the UAE (all you do is pay the customs fees and additional shipping). It is a great option to get things that you cannot normally get in the country and is very fairly priced, so it is definitely something to consider.

Is it hard to make friends?

Absolutely not! It is such a multi-cultural and international country that you will easily be able to find a group of people with similar backgrounds and interests. Also, because about 90% of the country is expats, most people are very open-minded and looking to meet people themselves. I was immediately surprised when I arrived how easy it was to meet great people, and I am sure you will be too.

What electricity outlets does the UAE have?

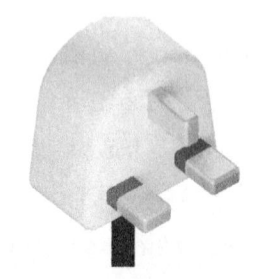

In the UAE, you will use a "G plug" - this has three rectangular pins in a triangular pattern, similar to what you will find in the United Kingdom. Most of the UAE operates on a 220V supply with a standard frequency of 50Hz, and I have had no problem using converters with European appliances (be careful if you have American appliances as you will need to ensure you have the right converters to avoid burning your appliances out).

Are scams an issue here?

The government does a great job at fighting scams and fraud, but unfortunately scams exist everywhere in the world. Luckily you can manage it by <u>never</u> giving any information out over the phone, even if a "police officer" calls you and threatens you. If this happens, say you will need to go into a station to talk to them. Be especially cautious about never giving out any text message codes as your bank accounts can be drained this way. Follow your gut here, if it does not feel right, it probably isn't!

What should you wear?

Both the climate and conservative Islamic moral codes call for some adaptation to what you might be used to wearing in the West. While you do not need to adopt traditional Muslim dress (it would be considered odd to do this), you should not go around with low-cut shirts or short shorts. Therefore, lightweight shirts and pants are highly recommended for warm weather.

For those in business, business attire is normally very formal and men should be ready to wear a full suit every day. For women, conservative and loose-fitting clothing is recommended. You should also ensure that you have high necklines and that everything down to your wrists and ankles is covered (luckily the UAE has great air conditioning!).

Can I drink alcohol?

Yes, you can drink alcohol. Contrary to much common misunderstanding, you no longer need any special permissions to do so. That being said, use discretion in your alcohol use as public inebriation can get you into trouble and is also culturally frowned upon. You can drink in select bars and hotels, and you will find liquor stores throughout the country (normally the windows are blacked out – so if you see this, it is probably a liquor store).

What are Fazaa or Esaad cards?

If you work in the public sector or with other participating entities (or if you have a Golden Visa), you will normally be provided with a subscription to either Fazaa (mainly Abu Dhabi-focused) or Esaad (mainly Dubai-focused). These are wonderful discount programs and you should definitely take advantage of them if you can!

Can I drink tap water?

For the most part, tap water in the larger cities is safe to drink and many people do so. Water in the UAE comes from desalinated seawater and groundwater, so I have sometimes heard comments that it tastes different, but I personally cannot tell any difference. That being said, many people still opt to install a water filter or have water jugs delivered weekly – I have a Nestlé water jug delivered every week (for about Dhs11 per bottle) and I have been very happy with it.

Is it true that there are no taxes?

One of the best benefits of being in the country is that it is a great place to save money. However, this does not mean that there are no taxes, as there are VAT taxes on goods, etc. But it does mean there are no income taxes, which still makes a huge difference for most people (be careful if you are American as it is possible you may still have to pay US taxes if you are living in the UAE).

INDEX

A
Airport 18, 19, 24, 39
Accidents 34, 53, 57
Accommodation 19-27, 41-50
Alcohol 15, 80
Al Barsha 26
Al Muneera 24
Al Raha Beach 24
Appliances 43, 79
Applications 74-76
Arabic 77
Arrival 18

B
Banking 10, 20, 28-29, 35-38
Bank account 35-38
Birth 66-68
Buses 59
Business Bay 25

C
Cable 48
Cars 16, 52-56
Car import 16
Car insurance 16, 53-56
Car purchase 53-54

Car rental 53
Car shipping 16
Childcare 68-69
Clothing 63, 79
Company-sponsored visa 11
Culture 60-64
Customs 14-15, 18, 78

D
Driver's license 31-34
Driving rules 55, 57-58
Dubai Marina 25, 27
Du 39, 49, 51

E
Education 65, 68-69
Ejari 45
Electrical outlets 78
Electricity 45, 48-50
Emergency services 55, 73, 86
Emirates ID 19-20, 29-34
Esaad 80-81
Etihad Rail 52
Etisalat 39, 49, 51

F
Fazaa 80-81
Families 65-70
Family-sponsored visa 11
Fertility treatment 67
Friends 78

G
Gas 45, 48
GCC Specifications 16
Golden visa 11
Green visa 12
Gyms 43

H
Health 71-73
Health screening 20, 31, 71
Health insurance 66-67, 71-73
Housing contract 45, 49

I
Identity card 19-20, 29-34
Insurance (see car, health, or moving insurance)
Internet 45, 48-50
Investor visa 13

J
Job-seeker visa 11
Jumeirah Beach Residence 26-27

Jumeirah Lake Towers 25-26

L
License plates 55

M
Maids 67-68
Mail 77
Maternity 64, 66-67
Medical tourism 73
Metro 26, 52, 59
Money transfer 36-38
Moving 9-10, 14-17
Moving checklist 9-10
Moving insurance 14
Municipality housing fee 48-50

N
Nannies 67-68

O
Orange card 54

P
Parking 57-58
Passport 9, 16, 30, 32, 36, 44, 48, 53
Pets 69-70
Phone plans 39

Police report 55
Pools 43
Post office 30, 77
Pregnancy 64, 66-67
Property rental 41-45
Property purchases 45-47
Public holidays 61-62
Public transport 52, 59

R
Recycling 51
Reem Island 22-23
Renting 41-45
Retirement visa 12

S
Saadiyat Island 23
Safety 55, 60-61, 63-64
Scams 43, 79
Schools 65, 68-69
Sewage 48-50
Shipping 9-10, 14-17, 66, 78
SIM card 39-40
Students 12, 65, 68-69
Student visa 12

T
Tamm 34, 76
Tawtheeq 45, 49
Taxes 10, 55, 81
Taxis 19, 33, 52, 58-59, 74-76
Temporary housing 19

Tipping 77
Tolls 56
Train 52
Typing center 30

U
UAE Pass 34, 44-45
Utilities 30, 48-51

V
Vaccinations 10, 68, 60
Vehicles 16, 52-56
Virgin Mobile 39, 49, 51
Visas 10-13

W
Water 45-50, 81
Women 61, 63, 64, 67, 80

Y
Yas Island 23

Emergency numbers in the UAE

- Police: 999
- Ambulance: 998
- Fire department: 997
- Coastguard: 996
- Electricity failure: 911
- Water failure: 922
- Your local Embassy: _____